ADOBE
PREMIERE PRO
QUICK START
GUIDE

NAVIN KULSHRESHTHA
ADOBE CERTIFIED INSTRUCTOR

First printing edition 2021
ISBN: 978-1-7376258-0-3

Writer: Navin Kulshreshtha
Book Design: Najdan Mancic
Cover Design: Najdan Mancic, Eric Brionez
Proofreader: Lauren Johnson
Skateboarder: Ryan Reese

BEFORE YOU BEGIN

Be sure to **download** the class media from the link below:

www.LearnPremiere.com/download/

You can also scan this QR code to open the link:

The link will give you access to the following resources for **free**:

- ➥ **Downloadable lesson files** so you can work through the projects in this guide.
- ➥ **Access to the Online Course** with interactive quizzes and **videos** that walk you through all the lessons step-by-step.
- ➥ **PDF summary** of the entire guide that you can use as a reference for your own projects.

TABLE OF CONTENTS

INTRODUCTION

Welcome to the **Premiere Pro Quick Start Guide**! The goal of this guide is to get you up to speed with Premiere Pro as quickly as possible, with minimal frustration and headaches. **Adobe® Premiere Pro** is one of the top video editing programs in the world. It's used by small content creators and big-budget Hollywood studios alike.

The problem is Premiere Pro can be complex and overwhelming for beginners. This guide seeks to demystify Premiere Pro by making it accessible for anyone who wants to learn it. It will lead you step-by-step from step one and show you how to edit a simple video and then export it. With some practice, you will be editing with confidence. I believe you'll ultimately find the effort to be worth it because Premiere Pro is a powerful piece of software that can do amazing things. And it is the industry-standard program for video editing.

"If you can dream it, you can do it."

—Walt Disney

 In case you're wondering, my name is Navin Kulshreshtha, and I'm a professional filmmaker and web designer. Currently, I live in Florida, USA and work with clients all over the country. My YouTube channel has a global following with hundreds of thousands of views. I'm also an Adobe Certified Instructor (ACI) and have taught hundreds of people how to use Premiere Pro. I am convinced that **anyone** can learn how to edit videos with some diligence and the right guidance. So let's jump right in and get started!

How to Use This Guide

"Nobody ever learned to swim by watching someone else swim."

—Navin Kulshreshtha

This guide is meant to be a **hands-on** introduction to Premiere Pro. That means you should download the media and follow along (see the link below). I also recommend silencing any distractions, like phone notifications, and dedicating yourself fully to the lessons here. For the average beginner, it will take around three hours to get through this entire guide.

Download Media

If you haven't already, you can download the media from the Learn Premiere website. Use the link below to get free access to the class media, step-by-step videos, and a PDF summary of the entire course:

www.LearnPremiere.com/download/

You can also scan this QR code to open the link:

After downloading you will have a Zip file on your computer named **Premiere-Pro-Quick-Start-Media.zip**. On many computers this file will be located in your **Downloads** folder, but it could be somewhere else depending on your settings.

Locate this file and follow these instructions to unzip it:

➴ On Mac, simply **double-click** the Zip file to extract the contents.
➴ On Windows, **right-click** the Zip file and choose **Extract All** and then choose an extraction location, such as your Desktop.

Once the files are unzipped, you should see a folder called **Premiere-Pro-Quick-Start.** Make sure you know where this folder is on your computer and can find it easily. If you want, you can place it on your Desktop or another familiar location, as we will be referring to this folder frequently.

📁 Premiere-Pro-Quick-Start

Figure 1.1

You will also need to have the **Adobe Premiere Pro** software installed on your computer, which is available at Adobe.com. Adobe does offer free trials and student pricing.

Now that you have the class media on your computer, let's get started!

CREATING A PROJECT

2

Before you start editing, you will want to get organized. Most video projects will contain dozens of media files, and large projects may contain thousands! So proper **file management** is crucial to keeping the project on track and keeping your sanity at the same time.

The best way to start a project is quite simple — create a project folder and place all of your media inside of it. For example, in this guide we will be working on a project about skateboarding. So we will work inside a project folder called **Skateboarding-Video**.

Step 1: Create Project Folder

Go to the **Premiere-Pro-Quick-Start** folder that you downloaded previously. Inside of this, you will see a folder called **Project-Folder**.

▼ 📁 Premiere-Pro-Quick-Start
  ▶ 📁 Project-Folder ◀—————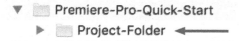

Figure 2.1

Rename this to **Skateboarding-Video**, which is a more descriptive name that will be easier to find as you work on your project.

Now your folder should look like this:

▼ 📁 Premiere-Pro-Quick-Start
  ▶ 📁 Skateboarding-Video

Figure 2.2

Skateboarding-Video will be our **project folder** and will contain all the assets, media, and exports related to the video project. The last thing you want is for your files to be scattered all over your computer because this will lead to chaos later on.

Step 2: Rename Media Folder

↪ **Inside** of **Skateboarding-Video**, locate another folder called **Subfolder**.

  ▼ 📁 Skateboarding-Video
    ▶ 📁 Subfolder ←———

Figure 2.3

↪ **Rename** this folder to **01-Media**.

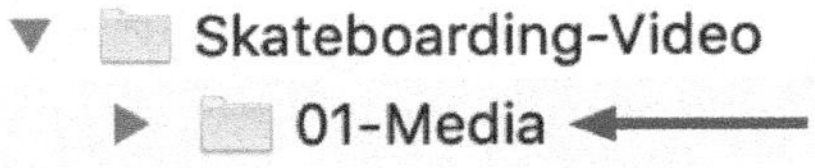

  ▼ 📁 Skateboarding-Video
    ▶ 📁 01-Media ←———

Figure 2.4

Step 3: Gather Media

The **01-Media** folder holds all of the **raw media** for the project, which are the source files for your project. Premiere Pro is compatible with all sorts of media files including:

→ video
→ audio
→ music
→ still images
→ graphics

Look inside the 01-Media folder, and you will see the raw media. In this project, I have already gathered the media and placed them in there. **For any of your future projects, you will have to do this yourself.**

Figure 2.5

Step 4: Create Additional Subfolders

➥ Inside the project folder, create 2 additional subfolders named:
- o **02-Project-Files**
- o **03-Final-Exports**

Now your project folder should look like this:

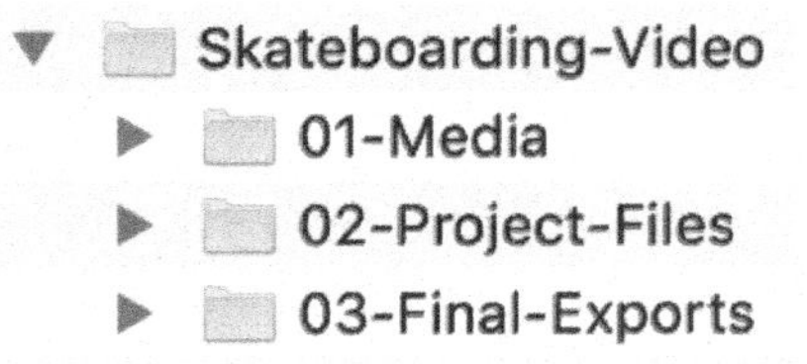

▼ 📁 Skateboarding-Video
▶ 📁 01-Media
▶ 📁 02-Project-Files
▶ 📁 03-Final-Exports

Figure 2.6

Every project that you work on should have structure to keep it organized. The first folder contains the raw media, the second contains the Premiere Pro project file (which we will create in the next step), and the third folder will contain the final exported video when we're done editing.

For complex projects, you can create even more folders. For example, I often create a folder for my graphics and another one for paperwork, such as scripts and legal contracts. Some editors like to have a folder called "research." It's up to you. The most important thing is that you have some sort of system to keep your project organized.

> ⬜ **NOTE:** I prefer to use numbers and dashes in my folder names but you can use whatever naming convention you prefer.

Finally, we're ready to jump into Premiere Pro!

Step 5: Create a Project File in Premiere Pro

➤ Start Premiere Pro and create a new project file by choosing **File > New > Project** from the top menu.

➤ Give the file name a descriptive name, such as **Skateboarding-Video-Edit**.

Figure 2.7

➤ Click on the **Browse** button and navigate to the **02-Project-Files** folder that we created in a previous step and save your file.

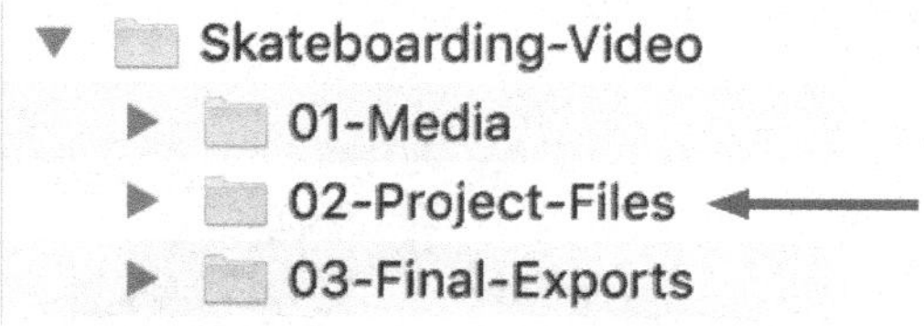

▼ 📁 Skateboarding-Video
  ▶ 📁 01-Media
  ▶ 📁 02-Project-Files ⟵————————
  ▶ 📁 03-Final-Exports

Figure 2.8

It is very important to save the project file to a logical, easy-to-find location because this file will contain all of your work.

Good job! You have created a solid foundation for your video editing project and are now ready for the next step.

INTERFACE BASICS

3

Within Premiere Pro, each of the little windows is called a **panel**. And the arrangement of all the panels on your screen is called a **workspace**. At the very top of the screen is the menu bar, which I call the **top menu**.

File	Edit	Clip	Sequence	Markers	Graphics	View	Window	Help

Figure 3.1

To begin, let's change the workspace. This will ensure that your screen matches the screenshots throughout this guide.

Step 1: Change Workspace

↳ From the **top menu**, choose **Window > Workspaces > Editing**.
↳ Then choose **Window > Workspaces > Reset to Saved Layout**.
↳ This will reset the workspace back to the factory original.

You are now in the **Editing** workspace, which is ideal for beginners.

The four main panels are called:

1. **Project panel**
2. **Source Monitor**
3. **Timeline**
4. **Program Monitor**

There is also a **Tools** panel with various tools for editing.

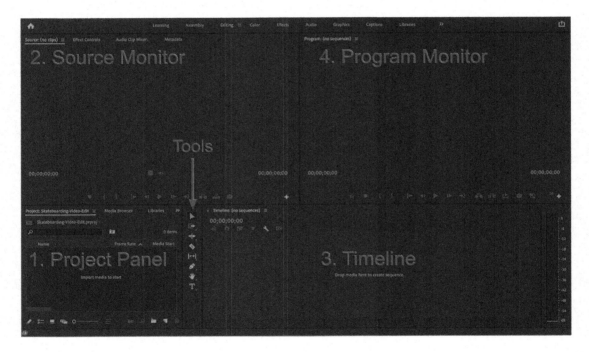

Figure 3.2

Don't worry about memorizing these just yet. We will cover each panel in detail as we progress through the edit.

> ▭ **PRO TIP:** If your workspace gets messed up, or you accidentally move or close a panel and get disoriented, you can bring your screen back to the default by choosing:
>
> ↳ **Window > Workspaces > Editing** from the top menu and then
> ↳ **Window > Workspaces > Reset to Saved Layout**
>
> This will magically bring your screen back to the Editing workspace you are seeing now.

The panels are looking pretty empty right now, so let's import some media and start editing!

IMPORTING MEDIA

4

All of our media files are inside the **01-Media** folder we created previously. Importing them is simple:

Step 1: Importing

➥ Choose **File > Import** from the top menu and browse to the **01-Media** folder. Select all of the media files. There are a total of **13 files**.

➥ You can use this handy trick: **click** on the first file then **Shift-click** on the last one. Then confirm.

➥ You can also try keyboard shortcut **Cmd+A** (Mac) or **Ctrl+A** (Windows) to **Select All** and then confirm.

All of the media will now appear in the **Project panel**. A single media file is called a **clip**.

> ▢ **NOTE:** Another way to import is to drag and drop the files from your computer's file browser into the Project panel in Premiere Pro.

At the bottom of the Project panel, be sure to click on the **Icon View** button, to make sure your screen will match the screenshots in this lesson. We'll talk soon about the function of this button and the other buttons.

Figure 4.1

The Project panel may be quite small on your screen, making it hard to browse the media files. So, I'll show you one of my **favorite** keyboard shortcuts in Premiere Pro:

Step 2: Maximize Panel

➥ Move your mouse over top of the **Project panel** and use the **Accent** ⌐ key on your keyboard to **maximize** the panel. This key is below the **Esc** key on most English keyboards, and shares a key with the **Tilde** character (~). If you are using a non-English keyboard, the Accent key may be in a different location.

Figure 4.2

After you hit the Accent key, the Project panel will become full screen. This allows you to more easily see your media files. You should see:

➤ 12 video clips name **Clip-01.mp4**, **Clip-02.mp4** and so on up to **Clip-12.mp4**.

➤ 1 music clip named **rock-music.mp3**.

Figure 4.3

At the very bottom of the panel are several useful buttons:

Figure 4.4

Go ahead and try them:

➔ Click on **List View** to show your media as a list.
➔ Click on **Icon View** to show the media as thumbnail images.
➔ Drag the **Zoom Slider** to the left and right to make the icons smaller or bigger.
➔ Click on **Sort Icons** to change the sort order (only works in Icon view) and then choose **Name** to sort alphabetically by clip name.

When you are in **Icon view**, you can visually browse through all of your media making it easier to find what you are looking for.

00;00;03;10

00;00;30;24

BASIC EDITING

5

Editing involves selecting your best media and placing it sequentially in the **Timeline** to tell a good story. Let's add our first clip.

Step 1: Preview Media

➥ In the Project panel, **double-click Clip-01.mp4**. It will open in another panel called the **Source Monitor**.

The Source Monitor allows you to **preview** your media before adding it to the **Timeline**.

The most important controls in this panel are:

➥ Playhead
➥ Playhead Position
➥ Mark In
➥ Mark Out
➥ Play/Stop
➥ Video Duration

Figure 5.1

Click the **Play/Stop** button to play the clip, or better yet, use the **Spacebar** on your keyboard. Then, do it again to stop. The **Playhead** will move through the clip as you play.

The **Playhead Position** shows the exact **time** within the clip where the playhead is located. As the video plays, you will notice the playhead position also changing, moving left to right. The **Video Duration** shows the total duration or length of the video clip. We will use the **Mark In** and **Mark Out** buttons shortly.

▷ HOW TO READ TIME

In video, time is measured using **timecode**. Timecode consists of 4 values as follows: **hours:minutes:seconds:frames**. So a timecode of **00:00:03:10** would translate to 0 hours, 0 minutes, 3 seconds, and 10 frames.

What is a **frame**?

You can think of a frame as a still image. Film and video are nothing more than a series of still images that flash so quickly in front of your eyes that they create the illusion of continuous movement. But in reality, they are just still images. Frames are easy to see when you look closely at a film strip:

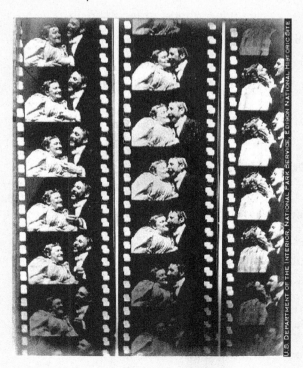

Figure 5.3 Film strips of "The Kiss," a film from 1896.

Step 2: Play Media from Beginning

➥ Use the **Up** arrow key (⬆) on your keyboard to go to the beginning of the clip. You can also drag the playhead to the beginning or use the **Home** button on your keyboard (if your keyboard has it).

➥ Click the **Spacebar** on your keyboard or the **Play/Stop** button to play the through the video.

In most projects, you will have much more media than you actually need. Nobody wants to see **all** of your media. Your job as an editor is to sort through the raw media and to present only the **best of the best** of it, and to arrange it into a good story. Remember — removing what's unnecessary is as important as including what's necessary.

To select a specific portion of a clip, we will mark **In** and **Out** points within it. This is how it's done:

Step 3: Mark In and Out Points

➥ Go to around **3 seconds** into the clip, which is indicated by the time **00:00:03:00**. It doesn't have to be exact.

➥ Use the **Mark In** button or keyboard shortcut **I** to mark the beginning of your selection. Then, continue playing the video.

➥ At around 8 seconds (**00:00:08:00**), use the **Mark Out** button or keyboard shortcut **O** to mark the end of your selection. Now you have selected a specific portion of the clip:

Figure 5.2

Since you have marked the clip from around 3 seconds to around 8 seconds, you have selected a total of around 5 seconds of the clip.

You can adjust the markers by dragging them, or you can clear them completely by choosing **Markers > Clear In and Out** from the top menu and starting again.

In Premiere Pro, you can move one frame at time through your video by using the left ⬅ and right ➡ arrow keys on your keyboard. This is useful when you want to mark a specific frame. Now, let's add the clip to the Timeline.

Step 4: Add Clip to Timeline

➥ **Drag** the clip from the Source Monitor and drop it into the Timeline.

Your Timeline should look something like the image below. Your clip may be larger or smaller than the one shown here:

Figure 5.3

Let's follow this same process to add another clip. But before you do this be sure that **snapping** is turned **on** near the top of the Timeline. This button looks like a **magnet** and should be **blue** to indicate that it is on. If it is blue then there is no need to click on it. If it is **gray**, then **click** on it so that it becomes blue like in the image below.

Figure 5.4

Step 5: Add Second Clip

> ↪ In the Project panel (where all of your media clips are), **double-click** on **Clip-02.mp4** to open it.

> ↪ Preview it in the Source Monitor and mark **In** at around **4 seconds** (00:00:04:00).

> ↪ Mark **Out** at around **9 seconds** (00:00:09:00).

> ↪ Then **drag** it into the Timeline. This time, be sure to place it immediately **after** Clip1. Since snapping is turned on, the clips should snap together like tiny magnets.

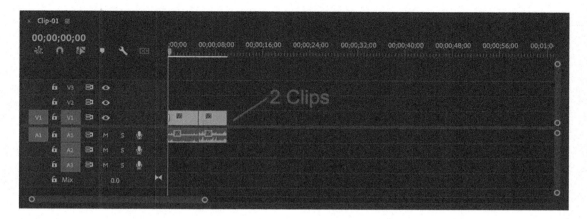

Figure 5.5

We often call these "video clips," but a more accurate description would be an "audio-video clip". The top portion of the clip is the video, and the bottom portion is the audio, which are **linked** together to form the complete clip.

Step 6: Add Another Clip

- **Double-click** on **Clip-03.mp4** to open it. Watch the clip.
- Mark **In** at around **3 seconds** (00:00:03:00), just before the skater comes on the screen.
- Mark **Out** at around **8 seconds** (00:00:08:00), after the skater leaves the screen.
- Then **drag** the clip into the Timeline. Be sure to place it right **next** to Clip 2.

Now there should be 3 clips in the Timeline, and you're starting to put a story together! Let's see how it looks.

Step 7: Play the Timeline

➥ Inside the Timeline, move the **playhead** to the very beginning. Here are 3 ways to do this:

○ **Drag** the playhead to the beginning of the Timeline. This technique can be slow, especially once the Timeline gets long.

○ Click at the **very beginning** of the **Time Ruler** near the top of the Timeline. Then the playhead will jump to where you click. This is faster.

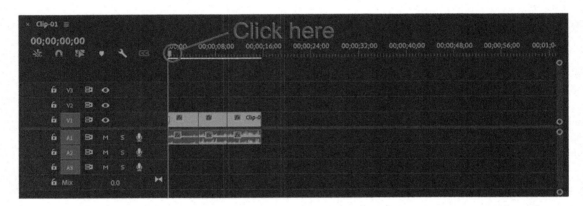

Figure 5.6

○ Use the **Home** button on your keyboard if there is one. This is the fastest way. However, many keyboards (such as laptops) may not have a Home button.

➥ Then, hit the **Spacebar** on your keyboard to play through the video.

The video will play in another panel called the **Program Monitor**, which shows the **edited video**. This panel is very important because this is what your audience will ultimately see when you publish the video.

At this point, you may feel that some of the clips are too long. We'll be fixing this in the next lesson.

Now you should be getting the hang of basic editing. On your own, add these 3 clips to the Timeline:

Step 6: Add 3 More Clips

→ **Clip-04.mp4**. Mark **In** at around **3 seconds** (00:00:03:00), and **Out** at around **8 seconds** (00:00:08:00). Add it to the end of the Timeline.

→ **Clip-05.mp4**. Mark **In** at around **4 seconds** (00:00:04:00), and **Out** at around **10 seconds** (00:00:10:00). Add it to the end of the Timeline.

→ **Clip-06.mp4**. Mark **In** at around **4 seconds** (00:00:04:00), and **Out** at around **8 seconds** (00:00:08:00). Add it to the end of the Timeline.

At this point, you should have 6 clips in the Timeline. Watch the entire video from the beginning to see how it's flowing.

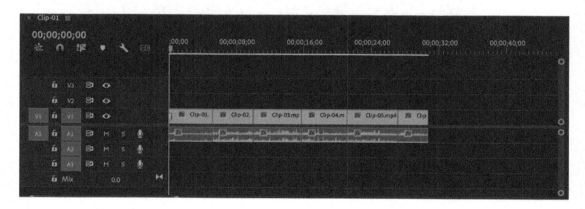

Figure 5.7

Good work! Your video may be rudimentary at this point, but you've actually come a long way. You now have the skills to assemble a simple **rough cut**, which is the first draft of your film. And you are now familiar with the four main panels in Premiere Pro and the basic workflow.

◘ TO RECAP:

1. The **Project panel** contains all your source media.
2. The **Source Monitor** allows you to preview a clip and mark **In** and **Out** points.
3. The **Timeline** contains all of your selected media.
4. When you play the Timeline, you will see the edited video in the **Program Monitor**.

Figure 5.8

Don't worry if the video is not perfect — in future lessons we'll learn how to polish the video, plus learn more about the Timeline.

REFINING THE EDIT

6

The Timeline is where your entire video comes together, one clip at a time. The Timeline contains multiple **tracks**, which you can think of as layers. There are 3 **video tracks** by default labeled V1, V2, and V3 and also 3 **audio tracks** labeled A1, A2, and A3. And there is a **scroll bar** at the bottom to help you move through the Timeline.

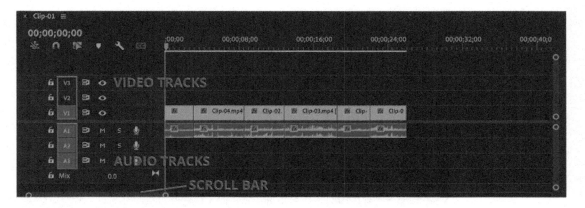

Figure 6.1

Here are some tips for making the Timeline easier to navigate:

Step 1: Increase Track Height

➥ Increase the track height of V1 by **double-clicking** the empty space in the track header.

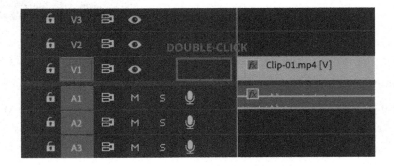

Figure 6.2

➥ Now the track will become taller, and you can see the clips more easily.

Step 2: Scrolling and Zooming

➥ **Drag** the scroll bar at the bottom of the Timeline to move left and right.

Figure 6.3

↪ Now **drag** one of the **zoom handles** (they look like circles) to the left or right to **zoom** within the Timeline. The zoom will also be toward or away from the **playhead** location.

↪ After zooming into the Timeline you can see the clips more easily.

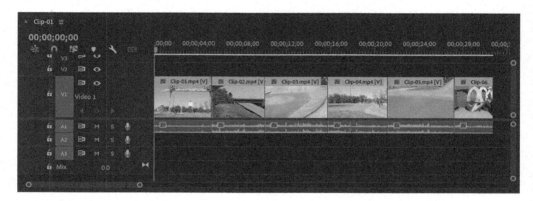

Figure 6.4

Get some practice **moving** and **zooming** within the Timeline since you'll be doing this a lot, especially as the video gets longer.

Now, let's learn how to adjust the clips in the Timeline.

↪ Some of the clips are too long, and we will **shorten** them. This is called **Trimming**.

↪ And some of the clips may be too short and could be made **longer**. This is called **Extending**.

The first clip in the Timeline **Clip-01.mp4** is too long (around 5 seconds), and we only need it to be around 3 seconds long.

Step 3: Trimming Clips:

➥ Be sure you have the **Selection** tool selected from the Tools panel. This is the default tool and looks like an arrow:

Figure 6.5

➥ Zoom into the Timeline so you can clearly see the clip names.

➥ Move your playhead to around **3 seconds** in the Timeline.

➥ Hover your mouse over the **very end** of **Clip 1** until your cursor becomes a **red arrow.**

➥ Then click and drag to the **left** to trim it. The clip will be shorter, and there will be a small gap in the Timeline:

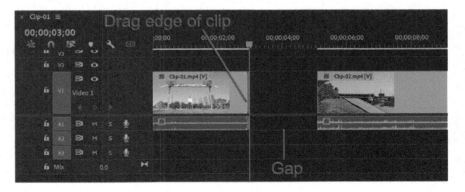

Figure 6.6

Step 4: Removing Gaps

➥ Remove a gap by **right-clicking** it and choosing **Ripple Delete**. If you don't have a right-click, Ctrl-click often works.

➥ You can also **click** the gap to select it and hit **Delete** on your keyboard.

Step 5: Trim Another Clip

➥ Now trim **Clip 2** in the same manner, but this time move the playhead to around 7 seconds (00:00:07:00)

➥ Drag the end of the Clip 2 to make it shorter.

➥ Delete the gap.

So far, we have only dragged the **end** of the clip, but you could also drag the **beginning** of a clip to trim it. On your own, see if you can trim both the beginning and end of Clip 3.

Now go through the entire Timeline and trim any clips that you think are too long, and remove any gaps.

Watch the video again to make sure you are happy with the length of your clips. Perhaps you trimmed too much and would like to make a clip longer. This is called **Extending**, and can be trickier than trimming.

Step 6: Extending Clips

➥ Go to the **last** clip in your Timeline, **Clip 6**, and drag the very end of the clip to the right. Now the clip will be longer.

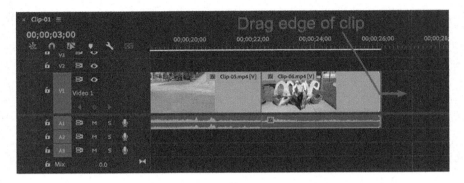

Figure 6.7

> **◱ NOTE:** You can only extend a clip to the length of its raw media source. So, if the source clip is 7 seconds long, that is the longest it can ever be.

➥ Drag it the other way to make it shorter.

➥ Now try extending the end of **Clip 5**. You will not be able to and will receive a message that the trim is **blocked**.

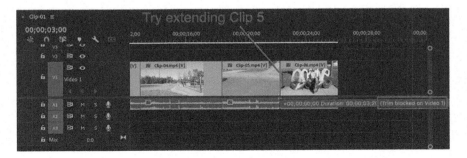

Figure 6.8

The reason is because Clip 6 is in the way and is **blocking** the edit. Before you can extend Clip 5, you must **move** Clip 6 out of the way.

Step 6: Moving A Clip

- ➥ Click the center of **Clip 6** in the Timeline and **drag** it to the right.
- ➥ Then, extend **Clip 5**, which should be easy now.
- ➥ Then, either close the gap or move Clip 6 back into place.

If you wanted to extend a clip in the middle of the Timeline, you would have to move several clips out of the way. For example, if you wanted to extend Clip 4 in the Timeline you would have to move Clip 5 **and** Clip 6 out of the way.

Step 7: Moving Several Clips

- ➥ Click on Clip 5 and then **Shift+click** Clip 6 to select them both. Shift+click will allow you to select multiple clips.
- ➥ Then, drag them to the right.
- ➥ Extend Clip 4 by dragging its edge.
- ➥ Drag Clip 5 and 6 back into place, or close the gap.

Be careful when you move clips around the Timeline because you can accidentally **overwrite** or **delete** other clips. For example, if you dragged Clip 6 **over** Clip 5, then Clip 5 would become overwritten. Fortunately, you can easily undo mistakes:

Let's change the order of clips in the Timeline now. Currently, the last 2 clips in the Timeline are Clip 5 and Clip 6. But what if you wanted to swap them? You can change the order of clips quite easily by **cutting** and **pasting**.

Step 8: Re-Ordering Clips

⮡ Click on **Clip 6** to select it and choose **Edit > Cut** from the top menu. You can also use keyboard shortcut **Ctrl+X** (Windows) or **Cmd+X** (Mac).

⮡ Move your playhead to the edit point immediately **before** Clip 5.

Figure 6.9

⮡ My favorite way to do this is with the **Up** (⬆) or **Down** (⬇) arrow keys on the keyboard. With these buttons, you can quickly move from edit point to edit point within the Timeline. (An **edit point** is the exact point where 2 clips meet.)

➡ Once your playhead is in the correct position choose **Edit > Paste Insert** from the top menu. Now Clip 6 should be **before** Clip 5.

> 🗋 **NOTE:** In this situation **Edit > Paste** would have **overwritten** Clip 5, which is why we used **Edit > Paste Insert**.

Moving clips in the Timeline is an important skill, so let's do it again.

Step 9: Re-Order Another Clip

➡ Click on **Clip 5** to select it and choose **Edit > Cut** from the top menu or keyboard shortcut **Ctrl+X** (Windows) or **Cmd+X** (Mac).

➡ Use the **Up** arrow key until the playhead is between Clip 2 and Clip 3:

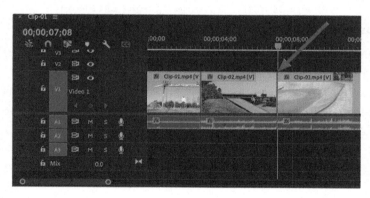

Figure 6.10

➡ Choose **Edit > Paste Insert** from the top menu. Now, Clip 5 should be **before** Clip 3.

Great work! You now have the skills to make clips longer or shorter, move clips around, close gaps, and re-order your clips. Watch the entire Timeline from the start and make any adjustments you would like.

Working in the Timeline can be tricky, especially once the video becomes more complicated. Keep practicing, and once you build up your skills you will enjoy having full control.

In the next lessons, we'll add some professional touches to the video including **music** and **transitions**.

⬛ TO RECAP:

1. You can **Trim** and **Extend** clips by dragging their edges.
2. You can delete gaps in the Timeline by **right-clicking** the gap and choosing **Ripple Delete**.
3. You can move clips by dragging them in the Timeline. Select multiple clips by Shift-clicking them.
4. To re-order a clip select it in the Timeline, then choose **Edit > Cut**. Move the playhead to another location then choose **Edit > Paste Insert**.

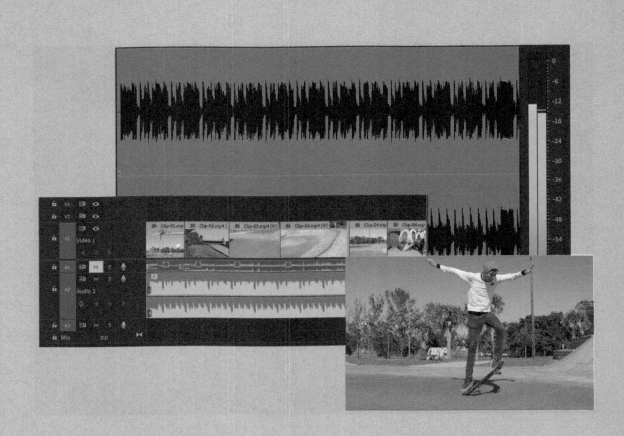

ADDING MUSIC

7

Music can completely transform a film or video project. It adds mood, texture, rhythm, pacing, and emotion. Premiere Pro is compatible with many audio formats, the most common ones being MP3, WAV, and AIF.

Step 1: Preview Music

➥ In the Project panel, **double-click** the music clip **rock-music.mp3**.

➥ **Play** the music in the Source Monitor.

Step 2: Add Music to Timeline

➥ From the Source Monitor, **drag** the music clip into the Timeline using the **Drag Audio** button.

Figure 7.1

➥ Be sure to drag the clip to the very **beginning** of **audio track 2**, which is labeled **A2**. Drag the music to the very beginning if necessary.

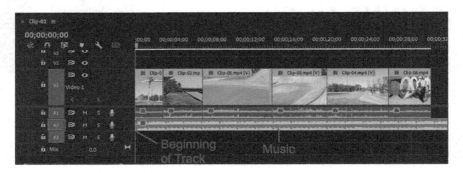

Figure 7.2

Play the video inside the Timeline from the beginning. You can see that music makes a big difference! But you may also notice that there's a lot of distracting noise in the background coming from the original video clips, so we will mute that.

Step 4: Mute Track

➥ In the Timeline, right next to A1 click on the **M** button to **Mute** the entire track.

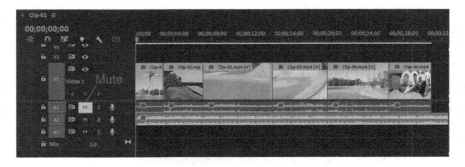

Figure 7.3

Now the background noises are gone, and the video sounds cleaner.

If you look in the Timeline, you'll notice that the music is longer than it needs to be, so we are going to **trim** the music so that it matches the video. This time, we are going to use the **Razor** tool to trim. Click on the Razor tool in the Tools panel to select it:

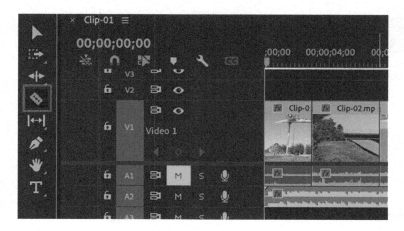

Figure 7.4

This tool does exactly what you think — it will cut or split a clip into two pieces.

Step 5: Trim with Razor

> ➥ Inside the Timeline, **click** with the Razor tool on the music clip to cut it.
> ➥ Be sure to click **just below** where the video ends, so that the music ends at the same time.

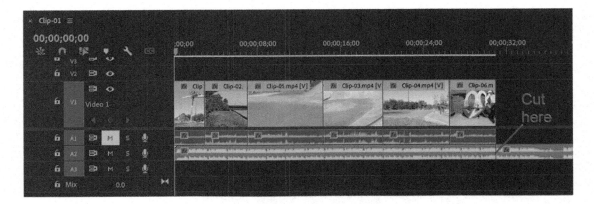

Figure 7.5

Now the music clip will be split into two clips, and we can delete the clip that is not needed. Click on the **first** tool in the Tools panel, which is the **Selection** tool (looks like an arrow).

Step 6: Delete Clip

➤ In the Timeline **click** on the extra music clip with the Selection tool.

➤ Hit **Delete** on your keyboard.

Now the music should end at the same time as the video. The music definitely makes the video more interesting, but it's too loud, so we are going to reduce its volume.

Step 7: Adjust Volume

➥ In the Timeline, increase the track height by **double-clicking** at the beginning of the music track. This will make the next steps easier.

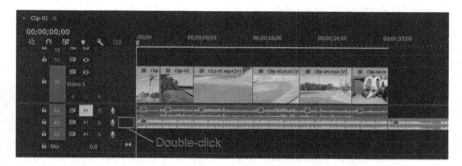

Figure 7.6

➥ In the music clip, locate the white line that goes across the clip. This is called the **rubber band**. It may be a little hard to see so look carefully:

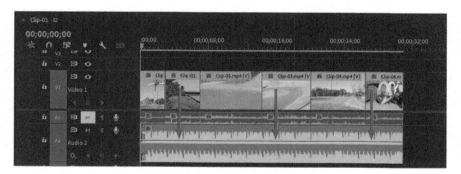

Figure 7.7

 ⟁ NOTE: If for some reason you can't see this white line at all, **right-click** the music clip and choose **Show Clip Keyframes > Volume > Level**

↪ Click on this white line and drag it **down** to around **-6 db**. Listen to the music to hear the results. Dragging this line down will decrease the volume; dragging it up will increase it.

Step 8: Avoid Clipping

↪ As you play the Timeline, observe the **Audio Meters** on the right.

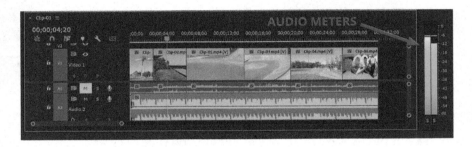

Figure 7.8

↪ This measures the **volume** level and uses a unit called **decibels (dB)**.
↪ The highest number on the meter is 0. You must make sure that your volume **never goes above 0 dB**.
↪ **Clipping** occurs when your volume exceeds 0 dB. The red lights will turn on at the top of the audio meters to warn you. If this occurs, simply reduce the volume of your music.

◘ GOOD WORK! In this lesson, you learned how to add music to your video, trim it, change its volume, avoid clipping, and clean up the Timeline. In the next lesson we'll make the video smoother by adding transitions.

ADDING TRANSITIONS 8

Go ahead and watch the entire video. It's coming along well, but is a bit rough in places. For example, the music ends rather abruptly and sounds unprofessional. Also, we could add transitions between some of the video clips to make the cuts smoother.

Step 1: Add Video Transition at Beginning

➥ **Right-click** the very **beginning** of **Clip 1** in the Timeline. Be sure to right-click the **very edge** of the clip and not toward its center. This step will be easier if you zoom into the Timeline.

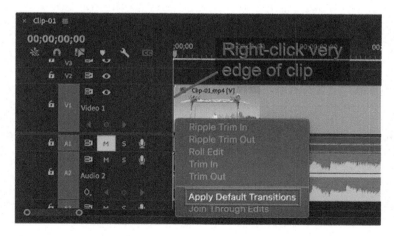

Figure 8.1

↪ Choose **Apply Default Transitions.** This will apply the **Cross Dissolve** transition, which is the default video transition. You will see it on the clip:

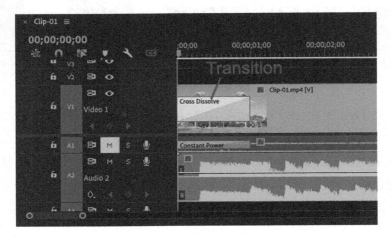

Figure 8.2

If you are having trouble seeing the transition, be sure to zoom into the Timeline.

Play the Timeline from the beginning. Now, the first clip fades in from black. Adding a transition like this creates a smoother start to the video. By default, transitions are 1 second long, which is often too much. Let's adjust it:

Step 2: Change Transition Duration

↪ **Double-click** the transition. Be sure to double-click the transition, and not the clip itself.

↪ A dialog box will appear with the current duration of 1 second (00:00:01:00). Change the value to **00:00:00:15**.

This represents 15 frames. Since our video footage was shot at 30 frames per second, 15 frames is half a second.

▷ DETERMINING FRAME RATE

Some common frame rates for video are 60 fps, 30 fps, 25 fps, and 24 fps. **Fps** stands for frames per second. You can determine the frame rate of your videos in the Project panel:

↳ Inside the Project panel click on the **List View** button.

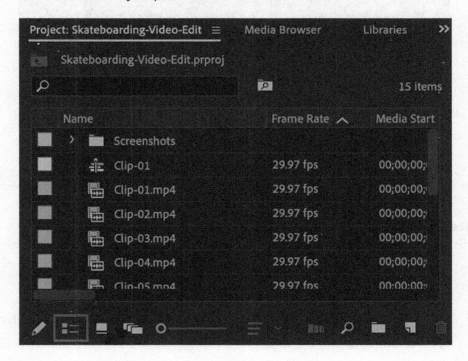

Figure 8.3

↳ Maximize the panel with the **Accent** ⏜ key on your keyboard.
↳ The **Frame Rate** column will show the frame rate of your video clips.

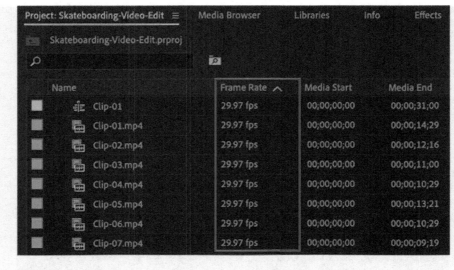

Figure 8.4

→ You may notice that the actual frame rate of these clips is 29.97 fps, but people often refer to this as 30 fps.

→ Click on the **Accent** [~] key again to minimize the Project panel.

Step 3: Add Video Transition at End

→ **Right-click** the very end of the **last** video clip in the Timeline. Be sure to right-click the **very edge** of the clip.

→ Choose **Apply Default Transitions,** which will apply the **Cross Dissolve.**

→ **Double-click** the transition and change the duration to 00:00:00:15, which is half a second.

The video now fades in smoothly and fades out smoothly. You can add a transition between the other clips if you want, but it's not required. Many professional editors would choose to have no transitions between the other clips because straight cuts often work just fine. A **cut** occurs when there is no transition between two clips and it switches instantly from one to the next.

Step 4: Add Video Transition Between Clips (Optional)

➥ **Right-click** the edit point between two clips and choose **Apply Default Transitions.**

➥ **Double-click** the transition and change the duration to 00:00:00:15 or whatever duration you choose.

Watch the transition to see if you like it. To remove it, simply click on it and hit **Delete** on your keyboard.

The music at the end of the Timeline ends suddenly, so we will add an audio transition so that it fades out gradually.

Step 5: Add Audio Transitions

➥ **Right-click** the very **beginning** of the music clip and choose **Apply Default Transitions.**

➥ **Double-click** the transition and change the duration to **00:00:02:00**, which is 2 seconds. Listen to it.

➥ **Right-click** the very **end** of the music clip and choose **Apply Default Transitions.**

➥ **Double-click** the transition and change the duration to **00:00:03:00**, which is 3 seconds. Listen to it.

Now the music fades in and fades out gradually. You can adjust the duration of the transitions to your liking.

Watch the entire video from the start and notice what a difference the transitions make. Now, the video seems more polished and professional and is ready to present to an audience. We'll learn how to export it in the next lesson.

🖸 **IN THIS LESSON, YOU LEARNED HOW TO**

↪ Add video and audio transitions
↪ Edit the duration of transitions
↪ Remove transitions
